Lynette.

CW00660464

Thinking Faces

FRONTISPIECE
*The drawing room at the Old Rectory
where Reynolds worked. His younger daughter
Emma in the armchair.*

Thinking Faces

PHOTOGRAPHS
1953 – 1979

JANET STONE

Preface by
IRIS MURDOCH

Chatto & Windus
LONDON

First published in 1988
by Chatto & Windus Ltd
30 Bedford Square
London WC1B 3RP

All rights reserved. No part of this
publication may be reproduced,
stored in a retrieval system or
transmitted in any form, or by any means,
electronic, mechanical, photocopying, recording
or otherwise, without the prior permission
of the publisher.

A CIP catalogue record for this book
is available from the British Library.

ISBN 0 7011 3302 3

Foreword copyright © Iris Murdoch
Introduction copyright © Janet Stone and Jonathan Gili
Photographs copyright © Janet Stone

Designed by Humphrey Stone

Photoset by Rowland Phototypesetting Ltd
Bury St Edmunds, Suffolk

Printed in Great Britain by
Butler & Tanner Ltd, Frome, Somerset

TO REYNOLDS AND OUR CHILDREN —
EDWARD, HUMPHREY, PHILLIDA
AND EMMA

Preface

The human face, that complex and significant surface, is the camera's most challenging theme. Janet Stone's remarkable collection of portraits covers the period 1953 to 1979 when she and her husband, the engraver and painter Reynolds Stone, lived at the Old Rectory, Litton Cheney, in Dorset. Janet and Reynolds were perfect hosts, and their beautiful house and huge wild garden provided a place of rest and inspiration for their friends, many of whom came to stay and work there, in the tradition of the 'reading party'.

Solitary concentration or social diversion were both freely available in that uniquely benign and generous scene. Janet, descendant of Elizabeth Fry, bishop's daughter, singer, developed her talent as a photographer, particularly a portrait photographer, after her marriage, when she took to photographing her visiting friends. She later became a professional; her work is in the permanent collection at the National Portrait Gallery, she has exhibited at the Royal College of Art and in other galleries, and includes the Duke of Edinburgh among her sitters. This book however is a story of her home, her family and her guests, a testimony to enduring friendships and continuing conversations, an evidence of capacity for happiness. The photos, mostly though not all taken at Litton Cheney, are also mementos of particular scenes and occasions, gatherings, discussions, festivities, trees, water, leaves and flowers, the seasons of the year, sun and snow, excursions, adventures, picnics by the sea.

During these many years Janet's visitors often met and knew each other, but without ever constituting a 'set'. A number of Bloomsbury faces make their appearance (for instance Leonard Woolf, Duncan Grant, Frances Partridge, Quentin Bell), but the visitors at Litton Cheney came from many 'worlds'. To list a few of the owners of these interesting faces: Kenneth Clark, Julian Huxley, Benjamin Britten, Lord David Cecil, Henry Moore,

Frances Cornford, Joyce Grenfell, Jill Balcon, John Piper, John Betjeman.

The book is not least a record of the Stone family, picturing Reynolds at his magical engraving in the corner of the drawing room, or painting beside a stream in the green light of the garden; also portrayed is the growing up of four handsome and talented children. Turning the pages of this chronicle of happy affections and varied characters we may often observe the same faces as they grow from youth to prime, or advance from prime toward a more mature wisdom. In the quiet centre is Reynolds, so brilliant, so gentle, so good, so perfectly present. On his death in 1979 the Old Rectory was sold. In this book of friendship one face, a beautiful one, is absent, that of Janet, who has preferred to stay behind the camera.

IRIS MURDOCH

Introduction

It was snowing in Cromer when I was born and it was also snowing at my christening in Davos – perhaps that's why I like snow so much. None of us know why I was born in Cromer, but my grandparents had a summer house there and my mother dashed back from Switzerland, where my father, Edward Woods, was being cured of TB in a sanatorium. We always thought it was simply because she was hooked on Cromer, but now I think it's more likely she just wanted me to have a British passport.

A month later my mother hurried back to my father in the Davos sanatorium and lost me on the way. She'd put me in a basket with a lid to it and she was desperately anxious to catch the train, which was practically moving. A porter was carrying the luggage, including the basket; he shoved it in somewhere, she got in somewhere else – and so she spent the journey rushing up and down the train until she finally found me under a seat, still asleep.

I was nearly two when the First War broke out. We were on holiday in England at the time and my father desperately tried to get into the war – it was a wildly patriotic time – but, because of his lung, he wasn't allowed to fight. Instead he became the padre at Sandhurst. I remember it vividly because I was so afraid for the prisoners of war in the woods where we went to walk with our Swiss maid; and at night, hearing the aeroplanes and knowing there might be a bomb. But Five the Square was a charming house. We were encouraged to climb the trees and I remember sitting in the laurel, watching my father play his mixed hockey in our garden with the then Prince of Wales, who became the abdicated King.

After the war my father was asked to be vicar of Holy Trinity, Cambridge, and so the next thing I remember was this eccentric house, Seven Brookside, where we kept our two donkeys. It was very Victorian, in a row, and we were frightfully snobby about being the best in the row. It never occurred to our parents to entertain us or anything like that, but the one thing we did once a year was go to carols at Christmas in King's. Everybody else went to a pantomime but we went to King's College Chapel. There was something very special about it, simply because this incredible Gothic building was entirely lit with candles, and the singing was absolutely perfect. I used to rush back to the attic and sing it all over again – though not with my parents within earshot. It was incredibly exciting, we thought – but then we were very unspoilt – we'd never been to a film or a play or a pantomime, and my mother, being ultra vague, never answered invitations for us to go to parties; I remember longing to go to one, or to a dancing class – that's what I craved for – but no.

We were all hopelessly shy as children; we had no school room so we had to spend our time in the drawing room, which was always full of someone waiting to see Papa, and there were always extra people at meals, which forced us to get used to other people. My mother, eccentrically, thought you ought to have your children at meals, so we were all there – all six of us – and one was pretty well obliged to have reasonable manners. If we didn't behave we were made to sit with our backs to the table, and as my brother Robin (later Bishop of Worcester) was incurably naughty his back was permanently to the table. I was painfully good – I was so afraid of people being cross with me that I went to extraordinary lengths, even to telling appalling untruths, not to be told off. One day we were playing mothers and fathers up and down the street, using the old pram – my poor sister Gabrielle (later Chairman of the WI) was pushed along in it as the baby though she had outgrown it some time before – and it occurred to me that it would be awfully nice to eat those chocolates in the drawing room; so I said to Robin, 'What about fetching us a few?'

He said, 'Of course,' and off he rushed. He brought some back and we gobbled them up.

'Do it again,' I said, and so he went again.

Then I said, 'Any left?' and he said, 'Yes.' So off he went again, cleaned the box out, and we were very pleased with ourselves. But when we came up the stone steps to the front door, there was my mother waiting with a tennis racquet in her hand. 'Come in,' she said. 'I know what you've been doing. Robin, come here.' And she beat Robin on his bottom with the tennis racquet and sent him to bed.

By then I was practically fainting with terror. She took me in to tea and said, 'Wicked Robin! But you, you deserve an egg, a boiled egg, for being so good.' I froze, and decided it was too late – I could never confess. And the egg tasted absolutely awful.

There was another occasion when I was faced with what I called bubble pudding – sago milk pudding – for lunch. I never could stand it, and – my parents were out, needless to say, or I wouldn't have dared – I simply put it down the back of the upright piano in the drawing room. It was never discovered, as far as I know.

My mother had a shocking temper and this always absolutely terrified me. My father had no temper whatsoever – his was the most angelic temperament I've ever known. This, of course, I much preferred. He was one of those serene characters who take everything in their stride. But he did take Mama's side, which annoyed us very much. They adored each other – they always sat hand-in-hand and they always called each other 'thee' and 'thou', which was a relic of their upbringing and their Quaker background.

We all went to church on Sunday morning. My father wore his gown and we trooped along carrying it as if he was in a wedding dress; it was rather a long walk, but we didn't have to go again and while he was at evensong we cooked buttered egg on the drawing room fire. It tasted so good – half burnt. My father took enormous care with his sermons – there was a beginning, a middle and an end, and they were all over in ten minutes. He had a wonderful voice, which had the most extraordinary effect on people. When we were in Cambridge you never could get a seat unless you went half an hour before. The same applied to Croydon, which was a vast church, big enough to be a cathedral – you could certainly get over a thousand people into it. When we were young my mother used to allow us to take a variety of books – they weren't all utterly religious – and we sat on the hassocks and looked back at the faces in the next row, using the pew as a table for the entire service.

Every holiday we either went to stay with our grandmother in Cromer or in one of the other houses. All the family – Buxtons, Barclays, Gurneys – had large houses, some of which are now guesthouses or hotels. So there were family picnics and family cricket matches and that sort of thing. We looked with grave suspicion at our cousins, because we only ever met them there and they all seemed rather more competent than us. And my mother used to change my hairdo to match theirs.

Of course we had no car, so we bicycled madly, even as much as twenty miles to Buntingford, where my Woods grandmother lived, who was Elizabeth Fry's granddaughter. There wasn't much traffic on the road, so it was quite safe. When my eldest brother Frank (later Primate of All Australia) became old enough to drive he said, 'We must get a car' – and indeed we did. That car – I shall never forget that car! It was a Morris Oxford and my mother thought it would be simple to drive it. We had a charming gardener called Haslop and she ordered him to sit in the front with her while she drove round Cambridge. She was so nerve-racking that he held his door open the whole time. They did get back safely, but she never tried again. The first time my father tried he careered down a hill and couldn't stop at the bottom, so *he* never tried again. But Frank drove us across France in this vehicle, which was open except for celluloid sides. My mother took a kitten in a shoe-bag and a stove on which she kept making tea. My father found it very hard to bear; he was always getting out and walking on ahead.

Usually, though, we went by train, and when we were very small my mother simply put hammocks across the carriage, or else we slept in the luggage rack. Meals on the train were agony for us because she would order three meals for six and then slop the food on to our plates. It was too bad – all in the aid of stinginess. We went to Switzerland a good deal because my father had the idea that one week in Switzerland was as good as twenty anywhere else, and that it saved everybody's life as it had saved his. The great idea was walking – we walked untold miles – and also reading aloud, which we did for hours. We were never allowed to be what's called idle, so we all drew, whether we could or not, while my father read us every mortal thing. My mother's passions were Cowper and P.G. Wodehouse; Papa's were poetry, *Pilgrim's Progress* and Dickens. It was wonderful.

School started exceedingly badly because I was sent to The Perse, where all the dons' daughters were, and unfortunately they could spell and I could not. So I was kept in all afternoon and I began to get an obsession that it was wicked not to be able to spell. I certainly fitted it into the Ten Commandments when they came up every Sunday and got more and more concerned that I was heading for some ghastly disaster. But just before we left Cambridge I was sent to a wonderful school in Great Shelford, where, for some reason, I could suddenly do everything that was wanted. I don't know what had happened to the spelling, but I found myself fairly well up in the form, and I was also alarmingly good at games, which was such a help, and at singing. I sang Nanki-Poo in *The Mikado* and I absolutely blossomed like a rose – just for a bit. That was a very happy time but it came to an end when I was thirteen and my parents moved to Croydon. We all dreaded Croydon – we thought it rather depressing after Cambridge.

I finished my day-school at seventeen on the dot because my great friend was going to a finishing school in Lausanne. I arrived a term late and everybody else could speak French but me. As I wasn't allowed to speak English all I could do was cry – I was appallingly homesick. I shall never forget it. But it's amazing what people can do, and one did rally, as they say. The most exciting thing was having my very long hair 'put up' for the first time by an incredibly sophisticated American girl. The school did at least teach me French, because we were put on our honour not to speak a word of English, and I never did, not one word, and before I had been there very long I started to dream in French. I was there the best part of a year; then I came home and got myself into the Royal College of Music. I had always sung, and it was always assumed that I was going to sing as a professional – which is rather odd, I think now, looking back. My parents weren't the kind of people who thought it terribly important for me to have a career; but they thought, 'If she's got to do something she might as well sing.' Mama was frightfully worried that I wasn't married, but they never worried about whether I was going to be a good singer – they never took it seriously. I had a particularly high, clear soprano voice – it was an inherited voice and my angelic brother Sam (later an archdeacon) had one too. We all played instruments – well, most of us did – and we were Handel and Bach mad. We had a family band; Frank was the cello, Papa the first violin and I the second violin. I can't imagine how it was my mother played the piano but she did – she was wildly unmusical, we thought.

It was so exciting to get away from home, and I enjoyed London terribly. I don't know that I would now but I did then. We went to endless concerts and queued up for the back seats costing 6d or whatever. The best bit of luck was getting a lodging in Cheyne Walk, which belonged to Rick Stuart-Jones. He charged me £1 a week and my parents gave me an allowance of £2. My elder sister Priscilla had said that that was quite enough to live on and I thought so too – I didn't mind being frightfully stingy. I lived on prunes and what we called 'Force', which was a kind of cornflakes. The room was minute – just enough space for a camp bed, an upright piano and a gas ring. It had a stunning view up the river with the barges. I walked to the Royal College of Music every day – I walked everywhere to save money – and of course I found it all electrifying. The people who took me up were Herbert Howells and Vaughan Williams. I went down to see Vaughan Williams at his house once or twice, and Herbert Howells came and played the organ at my wedding. The lessons themselves were extremely poor – my singing teacher was so bored with teaching it hurt – but I did a lot of singing with oboe obbligato and I knew all those wonderful Bach things and performed them in their hall. I had an amazing nerve in a way – I think you do when you're young. I sang at the concerts in the College without turning a hair, goodness knows how – I can't imagine doing it now.

I sang right up to the time I got married. The singing career was hotting up when I met Reynolds, but it never occurred to me to go on with it once I was married, partly because I hadn't got very far and partly because I thought looking after him was an infinitely better job – not that I thought of it as a job, but as a thing I wanted to do. And, looking back, I realise I should never have embarked on singing as a career because I haven't in fact got the right nerve. When it came to appearing on a professional stage I was terrified. I dare say I might have got more used to it, but I never did.

Much later on, after our daughter Phillida was born and before we had Emma, I went for an audition with a famous Italian teacher called Miele, and he was so excited he offered to teach me free if I came every day from Monday to Friday. He was absolutely set on my singing Verdi – he said nobody was better equipped to do it than I. So for three months I went up from Dorset on a Monday and came back on a Friday. In the end Reynolds and I both decided we couldn't really take it. I was photographing by then, anyway, and really Dorset was my work in life and I don't think I could possibly have taken on a second one. I was secretly rather glad when the singing came to an end, and Reynolds was more than glad – he couldn't stand my being away so much.

I met Reynolds at a party given by the Oppés, who lived along Cheyne Walk, and I said to him, almost on the second word, 'What about coming to a dance on Friday week with me?' I'd really got my mind on somebody else, whom I hoped to marry, but it was the end of the season and I did desperately need a partner for this ball. He didn't hesitate. If I'd known him better I'd have been amazed by the fact that he turned up at 94 Cheyne Walk in all the right gear, but he did, and off we went. He was an appalling dancer and he stood on my feet a great deal, so I said, 'Why don't we walk round the square?' Which we did. We spent the whole night talking and I remember putting in my diary, 'Well, he can't dance a step but he certainly can talk, thank goodness.'

We met in July 1937 and we were married in the following July. He needed a great deal of hooking in the end – he proposed several times and always took it back, which was too irritating, as I find it perfectly easy to decide on husbands, or houses, and he couldn't decide on anything, let alone a wife. In the end I went to Portugal with some friends of mine, and this rather stunned him. In fact it absolutely threw him. I hadn't been there a week when I had such a deluge of telegrams that I rushed back, abandoning my friends, and there he was on the quay. I said to myself, 'Fatal to hang about,' and we went up to Lichfield, where my father was now the Bishop. It was the first time Reynolds had ever met my parents – I'd kept him well away from Mama, in particular – and of course he loved them; but my mother, who was becoming really agitated by my not getting married, kept leaving us, hopefully, alone in the drawing room, which amused us very much. Reynolds could never find my father on his own, but he got him in the end, and my father said, 'Well, Reynolds Stone, can you support a wife?'

'I don't know,' Reynolds said. 'I've been earning nearly £700 a year.'

'Oh, that's more than enough,' said Papa. Then he said, 'Look, can you row?'

'Yes,' said Reynolds, 'I rowed for my college.'

'Oh well, that's absolutely splendid,' said Papa. 'There's just one other question: Is there any insanity in the family?'

'None.'

'Right,' said Papa. 'That's fine.' And my mother said, 'Oh well, let's all have some Horlicks.' There certainly wasn't anything like sherry in the house, let alone champagne – hard to believe now, looking back.

When war broke out Reynolds became a conscientious objector. The tribunal at Reading was a week after Edward was born and it was a very low moment for us – it was May 1940, Hitler was at the door and, because of Reynolds, most of our neighbours wouldn't talk to us at all. And of course Reynolds was worried that he'd made the wrong decision, as usual, only more so, and we went through all that purgatory as well. In the end he applied to go into the RAF, first of all doing photographic interpretation and then making models for the D-Day landings. He was stationed near Henley – that's when he got to know the Pipers so well. They were very sweet to him. He used to engrave in the Nissen hut between shifts, with people coming and going all around him; there was only one stove, the cold was awful, and he got bad jaundice at least twice. We were living near Reading, on Buckleberry Common, and he'd come over whenever he'd got half an hour, but he had to nip back because he was on eight-hour shifts night and day.

So I was alone, really, for pretty well four years. I practised my lute every day, which Dolmetsch had made for me – the old boy himself. At that time I honestly did think that I would sing professionally with a lute – nobody else, as far as I knew, both sang and played the lute in England. But it's an appallingly difficult instrument and I got frightfully sick of Elizabethan music, I must admit. I absolutely couldn't stick another note of it in the end. However, I practised away, while the poor children had to get on as best they could and we all prayed for the war to be over. None of us honestly thought we'd get away with it. We all thought Hitler would win in the end. It was a nightmarish time.

We had no car, so when I went over to see Reynolds I had to go by bus from Bucklebury to Reading and from Reading to Medmenham, and I too got to know the Pipers that way. John used to play my accompaniments – he's one of those extraordinary people who plays the piano by ear – and every time I went I sang; *The Magic Flute* mainly, and all the Mozart operas. And Myfanwy chipped in when the servant girl was on or something – she was nothing daunted. Philip Levi, who was an amazingly brilliant pianist, the best in the world for Szymanowski and Busoni, was absolutely mad about us as a family and he would also play my accompaniments. Once when he was staying with us the Betjemans came over and Penelope arrived saying, 'Well, I've brought my music.' She produced an album of Victorian music hall songs and put it on the piano. Philip looked at me in anguish, but he sat down and started to play; she stood up, and I have never heard such a ghastly noise in all my life. I laughed and laughed – the tears poured down my face. And then John got going too. How we guffawed! She said, 'I don't know what you're laughing at.' It was simply that her voice . . . I don't know how to describe it except that it was the funniest thing I have ever heard or seen in my life.

After the war we lived in Ashmansworth, near Newbury, but Reynolds longed to move to Dorset, where his family came from. We found the Old Rectory by chance one day while we were exploring Litton Cheney church. We looked over the churchyard into the garden and saw the house was obviously shut up; so we found the gardener, who was the spitting image of Noah, and he said it had been empty for three years. We peered through the window and thought it looked remarkably dim inside – everything was chocolate brown and rather depressing – but then we went round the garden. We knew at once that it was too incredible – nine acres of romantic ferns and rushing streams and ponds – and so we moved in. I'd got a barter cow in the war by exchanging some of Reynolds' engravings with Gathorne Hardy, who lived at Donnington Abbey and had the best herd of pedigree cows, and we had Myrtle and all Myrtle's offspring for nearly forty years, which meant one could make the butter and always have bowls of cream. So Myrtle had to be transported from Berkshire, along with the grand piano and a great many books.

But when we got there Reynolds had a kind of breakdown and sat with his head in his hands, saying, 'I've made the most appalling mistake.' And all the books sat about and not on their shelves for a long time. After that, though, he never looked back and refused to move from it. The house was a particularly nice one – it faced south and there was plenty of room for everyone; it was halfway down a hill and you could hear the water from the windows, the rushing streams. I remember thinking that the best rooms must be for visitors – it never occurred to me that it should be the other way round – and they came, almost every weekend, our friends. Reynolds wouldn't go away if he could possibly help it, so it was rather essential. He moved into the best living room downstairs, and no children were allowed in there unless they were old enough to sit quietly – I never, never in all their small lives allowed them in while Reynolds was working. But he did like his friends being there, and he liked me being there too, just listening to records mainly. We had crazes for things – we had a great Souzay time, and then Reynolds had a great Mahler time, which I couldn't take after nine in the evening. He also had an Indian time, which I found very funny; it used to irritate him, my giggles – he took it very seriously. But we did enjoy the same things – in fact I don't think he could have been more suited to me or me to him.

We had our visitors' book on the dining room wall, and everybody wrote their names on either side of the chimney piece. That was a great mistake, because it would be fascinating today, but of course I couldn't take it with me when the house was sold. The dining room also had a useful hatch – it was an enormously big one – and I used to go though it to the kitchen if people I didn't want to see came to the front door. One day somebody came in and saw me disappearing through the hatch but, rather like a camel's head in the sand, one couldn't see oneself so one presumed they couldn't see one either. My mother was even worse about that sort of thing. Once some people came to tea at the Bishop's Palace and she opened the front door and said, 'Oh no, you get a much better tea down in the town – here's two shillings.' Another time some people came to tea and she didn't a bit want them, so she said, 'Come and have a look at the garden.' They went all round this delightful garden, which had a moat in it and that sort of thing, and when they got to the kitchen garden door, which led out into the close, she said, 'And this is the way out.' They were dumbfounded; I met them the other day and they told me they really had been frightfully pleased at being asked to tea with the Bishop – he was the doctor and he'd got on his respectable suit and everything – and they arrived, expecting to have a nice tea in the drawing room and they were shown the garden door. Too awful! But my mother really didn't care what she said or did.

It was at Litton Cheney that I started taking photographs all the time. The people that we knew tended to rush to my albums, which were my sort of photographic diary. I've always had that kind of diary, since I was a child, and what I really wanted to do was capture the moment, like putting a butterfly on a sheet. When I was very young I was given a Brownie and I used to send the films off to Lightning Photographic of Torquay. They kept every single thing — they'd got a file which I never knew about until Iris and John Bayley drove us to Torquay once and they said, 'Are you really Janet Stone, née Woods? Would you like to look at your file?' And there it was — me from twelve onwards!

It was always the face that intrigued me so. I was particularly keen on profiles. But it was really only when friends started demanding dust jacket pictures that I decided to make a thing of it. Then publishers began asking me to go and photograph people who'd met or heard of me. It just shows how things get about, because one never advertised and one never didn't have somebody wanting to be photographed. I had three different cameras — a Canon, a Yashica and a wonderful old square Rolleiflex; they were all loaded and my great idea, because I think the face sets the minute people see a camera coming, was to start talking to get their minds off the subject and then take out the different cameras at different places in the room. The whole thing was over in twenty minutes, and it was far better than posing them at great length.

I used to go off for the day or the night and take people. I adored the contrast between, say, Lady Chichester in her siren suit and Henry Moore and his sweet sort of un-grandness. The greater they were the nicer, of course. And the friendlier. But the thing I didn't enjoy was hearing whether they liked the photograph, because nobody has the ghost of an idea what they really look like. Reynolds and I liked letters very much, but we were both nervous of the business ones, so he opened my business letters and I opened his. I minded very much when people said, 'Look here, I'd rather be smiling,' or whatever, and it was an enormous help to have Reynolds say, 'Well, I think that's a frightfully good photograph — nothing wrong with that.' And that's really one of the reasons I've been unable to take photographs since he died — the wish to do it went out of me when he was no longer there.

JANET STONE *in conversation with*
JONATHAN GILI

2. Back of the Old Rectory and Church

3

3. *Kenneth Clark, reading to our youngest daughter Emma in his library at Saltwood Castle. I first met him in 1947 when he and Benjamin Britten and I were godparents at Suzannah Piper's christening. 1958.*

4. *Edward Stone, eldest son. Went from working on French tankers in the Mediterranean to painting. 1960.*

4

5. *Phillida Stone, eldest daughter. She showed early drawing ability and, later on, became an illustrator and artist.*

6. *Humphrey Stone, second son who shared Reynolds' love of the country and became a typographic designer.*

5

7. *Lord Kenneth Clark,* 1964

8. *Emma Stone*, 1962

9. *Charles Lamb, First Sea Lord, over from Portland and playing duets with artist John Nash. He always had his own piano on board ship.* 1960.

9

10

10. *Ruari McLean, typographer; Mary Trevelyan, artist, and resident Litton Cheney pigeon,* 1961.

11

12

11. *David Jones, artist and writer.*
Never got over letting Petra Gill
slip through his slippery net. A
genius and a recluse who lived in one
room at Harrow-on-the-Hill. I,
absurdly, was trying to re-house him
at the famous Cavendish Hotel,
Jermyn Street.

12. *John Sparrow, Warden of All*
Souls, Oxford. He employed
Reynolds in the war to engrave
lettering for his book, Lapidaria.
Reynolds, a Pilot Officer in the
RAF, engraved in a Nissen hut
between shifts. 1960.

13. *L. P. Hartley adored rowing his*
boat on the Avon at Bath, but he had
grave swan troubles and his idea of
calming them with sleeping pills,
administered by his butler, failed,
I'm glad to say.

13

14. *L.P. Hartley*, 1967

15. *Frances Cornford*, 1968

16

16. *Iris Murdoch and her husband, John Bayley. We first met at David Cecil's, Cranborne. John was a pupil of David's at Oxford. 1963.*

17. *Mary Potter, painter. She swopped houses with Ben and Peter Pears at Aldeburgh: Ben's on the sea front and hers on the golf course.*

17

18. *Benjamin Britten, a meticulous player of games. Never talked music, except once in a London taxi when he suddenly asked, 'Can you think of a tune?' – the composer's nightmare, even for Ben.*

19. *Benjamin Britten. Though he and I were at the RCM together, we didn't get to know him till the first performance of* The Turn of the Screw *in Venice. It transpired that Peter Pears was a cousin of mine, if distant. Often at Litton Cheney, relaxing with Stones on the Chesil Bank or on picnics at Maiden Castle. 1960.*

18

19

20. *Imogen Holst*, 1973

21. *Benjamin Britten,* 1963

22. *Sir Peter Pears*, 1970

23

23. *Litton Cheney, Emma. Stunned by the charm of this beautiful churchyard, the view of the Rectory below framed in steep hills, and accompanied by the tune of rushing streams, little did we think then, in April 1952, that in the following April Stones would be living here and that, 27 years later, Reynolds' grave stone would be in this spot.*

24. *Winnie Jones said 'I'll go to Jan' at my father's death, and so she has been woven into our lives and we into hers for over 55 years; her iron routine, loyalty and love never failing; and Olive Myrtle joined the 'clan' in 1952, biking over from Puncknowle in all weathers to polish silver and scrub huge stone flags, and supply us with the local news.*

24

25

25. *Bicycling Stones, 1960*

26. *Emma and Anne Turner from next door, dressing up; future art historian and mathematician.*

26

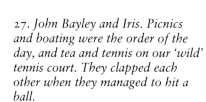

27. *John Bayley and Iris. Picnics and boating were the order of the day, and tea and tennis on our 'wild' tennis court. They clapped each other when they managed to hit a ball.*

28. *Emma Stone, the ideal model for me trying out new cameras. 1962.*

29. *Roger Hilton, artist, with Louisa, his mother. He was deeply shocked by Reynolds working in the corner of the drawing room of all places – unsuitable opulence.*

30. *Phillida in Louisa Hilton's Victorian clothes on New Year's Eve with deep snow in our Bride Valley, 1956.*

29

30

31. C. Day-Lewis and Jill (née Balcon) practised on the spare room piano when they weren't reading aloud to the assembled company, Reynolds engraving meanwhile.

32. Tamasin and Daniel Day-Lewis playing.

31

32

33. *Reynolds and Edward Stone*, 1963

34. *Chesil Bank bathers, icy water: Reynolds, Humphrey, Ben Britten.*

35. *John Hubbard, artist and American. We found a house for him near us on his marriage to Caryl, which was later sold to Christopher Sykes.*

36. *Rosetta Stone, my donkey Elizabeth Fry's foal, doing her best to kiss Judge Ian McIntyre, 1962.*

34

35

36

37. *John Nash, after planting the magnolia on the front lawn. Reynolds and he taught at the RCA once a week; many pupils for John, but almost no one for lettering.*

38. *Celly Clark and Humphrey. Celly's eye and easy conversation made her a special visitor.*

39. *Phillida drying her hair*

37

38

39

40

40. *James Lees-Milne, writer and pre-war friend, breakfasting in the library/ dining room. The hatch behind him several feet deep, through which one could bolt from unwanted visitors. 1963.*

41. *Emma and her friend Anne at sunset, on the island, 1963.*

42. *Derek Hill, bartered his drawing of Reynolds for this photograph.*

43. *Iris Murdoch and Reynolds. She affectionately understood Reynolds. He would happily break off work for her, even to staying away at Cedar Lodge, the Bayleys' house.*

44. *Father and daughter, Reynolds and Emma, on the top pond. Both Stones in looks, temperament, brains and devotion.*

41

42

43

44

45. *J.B. Priestley,* 1964

46. Zoltan Kodály, 1965

47. *Murray Perahia*, 1977

48. Joyce Grenfell, 1968

49. *Father and son, Reynolds and Humphrey, spider hunting.*

49

50. *Lawrence Whistler and Reynolds, two engravers on glass and wood. A stranger, Lawrence came with us on our camping trip to Venice in 1953.*

5

51. *John Betjeman. We first met with John Piper in Reading, looking at Victoriana, in 1948. He sits, to his delight, in the tennis pavilion by the Victorian glass window banned from the rectory by the late Rector of Litton Cheney.*

51

52

52. *Stanley Morison, famous designer, typographer and writer of* The History of The Times. *He employed Reynolds to engrave the masthead for* The Times.

53. *Lawrence Whistler*, 1973

54. *Sir John Betjeman*, 1973

55. *John Piper*, 1964

56. *Myfanwy Piper*, 1964

57. *John Sparrow, a typographical expert and book collector. At Winchester, K. Clark and he met at the drawing school where they took their art work very seriously indeed.*

57

58. *Geoffrey and Margaret Keynes. Geoffrey, a brother of Maynard, surgeon and book collector; Margaret, a sister of Gwen Raverat of* Period Piece *fame and née Darwin.*

58

59. *Reynolds on his way to paint in the Dell; the gothic arch a sop to my 'gothic mania'.*

60. *Tom Pile, superb gardener. His broad Dorset dialect made him difficult to understand. He was devoted to 'the little maid', as he called Emma.*

59

60

61. *C. Day-Lewis and Daniel in the boat used for after-luncheon coffee parties. Once plied between Bridport Harbour and Lyme Regis.*

61

62

63

62. Viscount Montgomery, teasing Liddell-Hart who, though madly distinguished, was 'only a captain'. After photographing him lunch at his special table in Claridges, on a little curtained platform. Good food and a lecture on the art of war.

63. C. Day-Lewis and Mary Moore (Henry's daughter), Humphrey, Emma and Reynolds.

64. *Kathleen and Basil Liddell-Hart, the tank and amateur fashion expert! Kathleen beautifully conformed to his ideal of elegance and tiny waists. We first met him when my father was Bishop of Croydon.*

65. *A Chesil Bank picnic with Celly Clark, Juliette Huxley, Caryl Hubbard, Bruce Whineray, Julian Huxley.*

66. *Juliette Huxley, dazed after Julian flees to leave 'frail females' to face the large local bull alone.*

67. *Captain Liddell-Hart*, 1964

68. *C. Day-Lewis,* 1970

69. *Sir Julian Huxley*, 1965

70. Professor John Bayley, 1972

71–73. *Reynolds would
not hurt a woodlouse, let
alone a flea.*

74

75

75. *Reynolds and Stanley Morison, who rarely left the metropolis if he could help it, but did come to look at Reynolds' lettering, cut in our stables, on the giant marble memorial to Winston Churchill for Westminster Abbey.*

74. Above *Reynolds polishes the marble.*

76. *David Jones*, 1966

77. Stanley Morison, 1964

78

78. *Rachel, wife of Lord David
Cecil, played with Reynolds at
Eton. She was a granddaughter
of the headmaster, Francis
Warre-Cornish, and Reynolds'
father was a housemaster there.*

79. *Lord David Cecil, writer and
Oxford don*

79

80. *The Duchess of Devonshire (Debo) looking at my photographic diary. We got to know her through Reynolds' work for her.*

80

81

81. *Siegfried Sassoon and the longest legs I ever encountered. The talk was mainly of Eton days; he knew Reynolds' housemaster father.*

82. *Lord David Cecil, 1966*

83. *Robin Whistler*, 1966

84. *Barbara Griggs, journalist, and the Mini Moke I used as a 'horse' over hill and dale and collecting more stones from the Chesil Bank for my pebble path in the rose garden.*

85. *Warren Benbow, Commander R. N. and godson, over from Yeovil. Trained as helicopter pilot along with HRH Prince of Wales.*

86. *Mr Pitcher, taximan, who drove Emma in his ancient car to the dancing class lying on the floor hoping not to be seen.*

87. *John Bayley, the cleverest and most entertainingly versatile of men, remaking his trousers with copydex and inventor of interesting food and drink.*

88. *L. P. Hartley outside the old family office near Peterborough.*

89. *Brothers Frank, Archbishop of Melbourne and Robin, Dean of Windsor, well used to officiating at family weddings.*

84

85

86

87

88

89

90. *Professor John Bayley*, 1970

91. *Dame Iris Murdoch*, 1966

92

92. *Reynolds most unhappily in a train. Found travelling pure purgatory, even on our honeymoon; he never took a holiday if he could help it, certainly not* abroad.

93. *Reynolds broke off from engraving morning and evening to paint every afternoon, wet or fine; 'Married to trees', we joked.*

94. *John Rothenstein, head of the Tate Gallery, 1966.*

95. *C. Day-Lewis on one of our train picnics on the branch line from Bridport to Maiden Newton where Sylvia Townsend Warner, in gloves and hat, met us for tea on the train.*

96. *The C. Day-Lewises' beloved Citroën and typical sense of humour.*

93

94

95

96

97

98

99

97. *Jenni Stone, née Orme, ex-daughter-in-law, beautiful and clever, so horse mad she kept a horse in London.*

98. *V.S. Pritchett and Dorothy, in his moustache year, banned as far as photographs went by his publisher Norah Smallwood of Chatto & Windus.*

99. *Jonathan Gili, film director, publisher and son-in-law; Reynolds, Jenni, Emma, Phillida and Solveig.*

100. *Stan Lawrence at his workshop in Bleeding Heart Yard, E.C.4, where he taught Reynolds, aged 22, to hold an engraving tool and for 50 years supplied him with boxwood to engrave upon.*

100

101. *Harold Abrahams, athlete of* Chariots of Fire *fame, for whom I had my first crush when I was 12. He was one of many Cambridge undergraduates who used to come to Sunday breakfast in my parents' house.*

101

102. *Phillida Stone*, 1965

103. *Jonathan Gili,* 1963

104. *Sir Compton Mackenzie*, 1963

105. *Gabrielle Pike*, 1963

106. *Emma, 1968*

106

107. *Edward Stone*

107

108. *William Plomer*, 1969

109

109. *The Marchioness of Salisbury, a very beautiful, perceptive and caring friend.*

110. *Reynolds, Pat Trevor-Roper, Desmond Shawe-Taylor, Jack Rathbone, Dadie Rylands and Raymond Mortimer.*

111. *Billy Henderson and Frank Tait, painter and doctor.*

112. *Raymond Mortimer*

110

111

112

113. *Julian Bream,* 1973

114. *The Marchioness of Salisbury, 1971*

115. *Reynolds Stone*, 1973

116. P.J. Conkright,
typographer, from the
Princeton University Press, and
Reynolds.

117. The Bayleys and Reynolds,
relaxing.

118. *Frances Partridge*, 1973

119. *Raymond Mortimer*, 1971

120

121

122

12

120. *Edward Hussey, Fellow of All Souls, reputed to be the only scholar passing the interview into All Souls without uttering a word, his written work was so brilliant. We first met him in Venice in 1965.*

121. *Robert Birley, Headmaster of Eton. His feet flapped in the wind as he walked across court, and clever at spotting interesting pupils he invited to breakfast.*

122. *Joseph Losey, film director*

123. *Norah Smallwood of Chatto & Windus bravely stays in the attic room one Christmas. We were 17 souls, I remember, and everyone had a stocking.*

124. *Dadie Rylands, Reynolds and Jim Lees-Milne.*

125. *Edward Hussey*, 1971

126. *Christopher Sykes,* 1972

127. *Duncan Grant,* 1966

128. *Leonard Woolf*, 1966

129

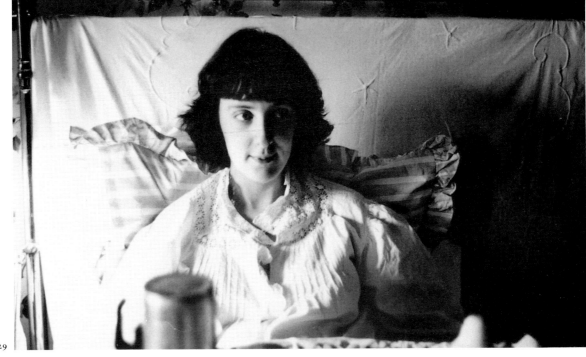

130

129. *Solveig Stone, daughter-in-law, obeying the breakfast in bed rule to the tune of a bedroom coal fire, relit as I came in with the tray.*

130. *Reynolds, who rarely got off his engraving nest except for Iris and John who luckily for us stayed fairly often, year after year.*

131. *Viscount Esher, architect, photographed when head of the RCA.*

132. *John Sparrow is talking to Eddy Sackville, West.*

131

132

133. *Dr George Tee, bacteriologist, plate camera and printing enthusiast, who lived over the hill at Cerne Abbas.*

133

134

135. *Stephen Spender*

134. *Lord Adrian of Trinity College, Cambridge. His suggestion of standing in the bath for the best photographic light not a success, but the session proved to me that the really great are the nicest and easiest people to photograph.*

136. Henry Moore, 1970

137

137. *Lunch on a summer day: Solveig, Humphrey, Reynolds and Edward Hussey.*

138. *Angelica, granddaughter.*

139. *Sylvia Townsend Warner at Maiden Newton. Coal black coffee and cigarette and, for me, a coat over the knees against her clawing cats.*

140. *Reynolds, Solveig, Humphrey and snowing, in front of the porch Litton Cheney.*

141. *Grandchildren – Angelica, Oliver, Daisy and Emily Stone.*

138

139

140

141

142. *The Dowager Marchioness of Cholmondeley, 1971*

143. *Humphrey Stone*, 1961

144. *Edward Stone*, 1973

145. *Sylvia Townsend Warner, 1970*

146. *Dame Freya Stark at Litton Cheney from Asolo.*

147. *Harold Macmillan at the Encaenia, All Souls College.*

148. *Ian Beck, artist and son-in-law and Emma.*

149. *Kenneth Clark, 1977, at Litton Cheney.*

148

149

150. *Dame Freya Stark*, 1969

151. *Sir Roy Harrod, 1973*

152. *Wilfred Thesiger, 1971*

153. *Edward Ardizzone, 1964*

154

155

154. *Reynolds and Phillida printing 'The Old Rectory' engravings, commissioned by Warren Editions, on one of the 12 presses in the barn.*

155. *Daisy Gili, granddaughter*

156. *David Game. Gifted and clever; a kind and constant family friend.*

157. *John Sparrow, and tea cosy, working in his bedroom.*

158. *Angelica Stone, granddaughter.*

159. *Sir Steven Runciman*, 1973

160. *Emma*

161. *Reynolds in the Dell. We cultivated and loved tunnels of trees.*

162. *Sir David Piper*, 1973

163. *Cyril Connolly, 1972*

164

165

164. *Duke of Edinburgh, Buckingham Palace. Ice broken when HRH discovered who my parents were. They must have been amongst his most eccentric acquaintances.*

165. *Cecil Beaton, taken at his (alarming) request, 1978.*

166. *Reynolds and Diana Cooper, at Firle, Lewes, where Reynolds painted the commission to join a roomful of 'Firle' artists' pictures.*

167. *Quentin Bell and Reynolds mending my specs.*

166

167

168. Emma Stone, 1962

169. Reynolds reading aloud

Index

Lynette